The Year in History
1992

Whitman Publishing, LLC

Scan the QR code at left or visit us at www.whitman.com for a complete listing of collectibles-related books, supplies, and storage products.

Whitman®

Contents

Introduction

The year 1992 is both close to us and yet strangely distant. So much of that year still seems immediate, like the presidential race that first brought Bill Clinton to the White House, and the rise of reality television that began with MTV's series *The Real World*. *The Simpsons* was already well established on television, and it's going strong today. Then as now, movie theaters showed superhero movies *(Batman Returns)*, *Saturday Night Live* alumni projects *(Wayne's World)*, animated Disney family fare *(Aladdin)*, and Woody Allen films *(Husbands and Wives)*. The stars included Robert Downey Jr., Tom Cruise, Eddie Murphy, Ralph Fiennes, and Sandra Bullock. Wal-Mart had established itself as a commercial force to be reckoned with: the chain comprised more than 1,700 stores across 40 states, and had surpassed Sears, Roebuck in sales. Founder Sam Walton died on April 5 of that year, but the chain he founded was already well on its way to its current status as the world's biggest retailer.

In other ways, 1992 was sowing the seeds for the reality of 2012. Debit cards and automated teller machines (ATMs) were beginning to gain a foothold, even though we were still a long way from swiping our debit cards to make purchases at stores and gas stations as a matter of course. Likewise, home video games were becoming more sophisticated, with the first forays into survival-horror and real-time strategy games, and the rivalry between different companies' systems was a throwback to the VHS-Betamax war of the 1980s. The introduction of Mortal Kombat prompted parental outcry about violence in video games, which led to the founding of the Entertainment Software Rating Board—and ironically to even more video-game violence, since makers could now simply put an M (for Mature) rating on a game without fear of repercussions.

Yet in other ways the world *has* changed greatly since then. Personal computers were prevalent in 1992 but not yet taken for granted as part of our everyday lives, and the Internet had not yet become a constant presence in the life of most Americans. Most of us never would have imagined that 20 years in the future we would have computers small enough to carry in our pockets that would send and receive phone calls, electronic mail, and information gathered from all over the world and connected invisibly in the ether.

We were still learning how to program our VCRs to record our favorite TV shows (and the introduction in November of the VCR+ system went a long way toward making that easier). The digital media revolution was a long way off, despite the presence of compact discs for our music. (Die-hard vinyl loyalists were still common.) Mobile phones were still the exception rather than the rule; they carried a certain status, since it seemed to be primarily the rich and important movers and shakers who owned them. The rest of us? We still had to worry about choosing a long-distance carrier. In the field of popular music, we still had Michael Hutchence (INXS), Whitney Houston, Kurt Cobain, and Michael Jackson.

Looking back at 1992 gives us much food for thought. We can't help but think about the people and things we've lost; yet, at the same time, comparing our world then and now, we are struck by how far we've come. The breathtaking speed at which technology develops and evolves gives us so many advantages now that we didn't possess in 1992. Enjoy this look back at our shared past, with all its drama and delight—and don't be surprised when the moments captured in these pages summon up memories of your own.

As comfortable behind a microphone as she is in front of a camera, actress and singer Selena Gomez is born on July 22. This photo shows her at the 6th Annual Hollywood Style Awards in Beverly Hills on October 10, 2009.

Famous People Born in 1992

The generation born in 1992 has not had much time in which to make its mark. In years to come we'll probably look back at this list and be amazed by the scientists, innovators, politicians, and writers who weren't represented here because their careers had not yet gotten off the ground. Because film and television actors and singers often begin their professional lives quite early and are often in the public eye from a relatively young age, they are strongly represented here. Television programming for young people has become so ubiquitous that young actors, singers, and dancers can be show-business veterans by the time they reach adulthood. Among the many actors here who started their careers as child stars are Miley Cyrus (November 23), Selena Gomez (July 22), Freddie Highmore (February 14), Malcolm David Kelley, (May 12), and Nick Jonas (September 16).

Similarly, because athletes tend to peak sooner than people in less physically demanding work, they also tend to come to prominence earlier, and athletic achievers comprise a significant number of the names here.

Another prominent category is the children of celebrities. Many of our favorite actors and singers who came to prominence in the 1980s had children in 1992, among them Belinda Carlisle of the Go-Go's, award-winning country music phenomenon Garth Brooks, John Travolta *(Look Who's Talking, Pulp Fiction)*, and Will Smith *(I, Robot; The Pursuit of Happyness)*. Although their 1992 offspring may be known now mainly for their famous parents, in years to come it will be interesting to see what mark they make on the world in their own right.

Future singer and star of the popular show *Sonny With a Chance* Demi Lovato is born on August 20. Here she is shown at the premiere of *Hannah Montana: The Movie* in April 2009.

January 1—Jack Wilshere, English footballer

January 19—Logan Lerman, actor *(Percy Jackson & the Olympians: The Lightning Thief)*

January 19—Shawn Johnson, Olympic medalist in artistic gymnastics and *Dancing With the Stars* winner

January 19—Mac Miller (b. Malcolm McCormick), rapper *(Blue Slide Park)*

January 25—Olivia Bonilla, singer-songwriter *(Arrival)*

January 26—Cassidy Lehrman, actress *(Entourage)*

February 2—Rebop Rundgren, son of rockers Todd Rundgren and Michele Rundgren *(née* Gray)

February 5—Neymar (b. Neymar da Silva Santos Júnior), Brazilian soccer player

February 7—Miguel Andres Matienzo Guerra, Mexican athlete

February 11—Taylor Lautner, actor *(Twilight)*

February 11—Blair Dunlop, English actor *(Charlie and the Chocolate Factory)*

February 14—Freddie Highmore, English actor *(Charlie and the Chocolate Factory)*

February 17—Meaghan Jette Martin, singer and actress *(Camp Rock)*

February 18—Logan Miller, musician and actor *(Ghosts of Girlfriends Past)*

February 18—Melinda Shankar, Canadian actress *(How to Be Indie)*

February 25—Max Aaron, 2011 U.S. national junior champion figure skater

March 4—Jazmin Grace Grimaldi, daughter of Albert II, prince of Monaco

March 7—Bel Powley, English actress *(M.I. High)*

March 8—Charlie Ray, actress *(Little Manhattan)*

March 10—Emily Osment, singer and actress *(Spy Kids 2, Hannah Montana)*

March 14—Jasmine Murray, singer and *American Idol* finalist

March 17—Eliza Bennett, English singer and actress *(Inkheart)*

March 19—Henry and Angus Bernsen, twin sons of actors Corbin Bernsen and Amanda Pays

March 22—Luke Freeman, English footballer

March 23—Kyrie Irving, Australian-American basketball player (Cleveland Cavaliers)

March 26—Haley Ramm, actress *(X-Men: The Last Stand)*

April 8—Shelby Young, television and film actress *(American Horror Story, The Social Network)*

April 12—Giorgio Cantarini, Italian actor *(Life Is Beautiful)*

April 13—Jett Travolta (d. 2009), daughter of John Travolta and Kelly Preston

April 16—Prince Sébastien of Luxembourg, prince of Luxembourg

April 24—Larramie "Doc" Shaw, actor and rapper *(Tyler Perry's House of Payne)*

April 27—James Duke Mason, son of singer Belinda Carlisle and Morgan Mason

May 4—Ashley Rickards, actress *(Awkward)*

May 4—Courtney Jines, actress *(The War at Home)*

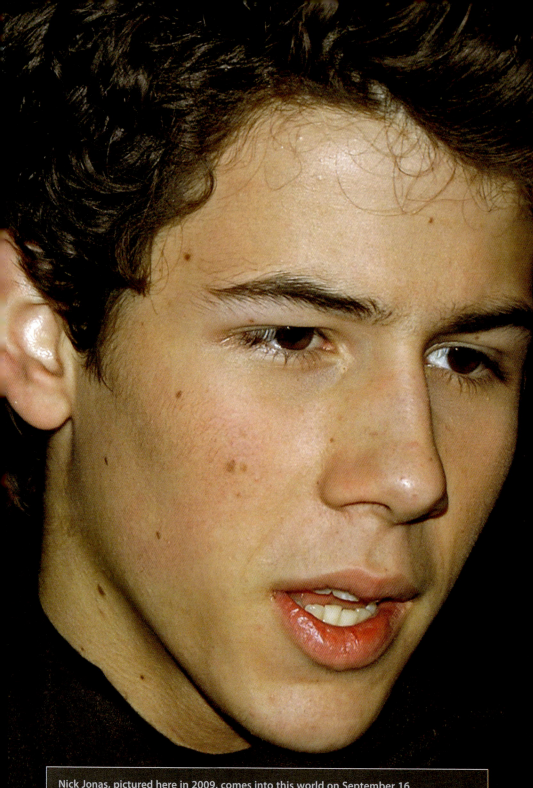

Nick Jonas, pictured here in 2009, comes into this world on September 16. The multitalented performer appears on Broadway by age 7 and forms the highly popular musical act The Jonas Brothers, with his brothers, at the age of 12.

May 12—Malcolm David Kelley, actor *(Lost)*

May 16—Gavin Hetherington, English actor and dancer

May 18—Spencer Breslin, actor *(The Happening)* and musician

May 18—Josh Phelps, soccer player

May 21—Olivia Olson, singer and actress *(Love Actually)*

May 21—Hutch Dano, actor *(Zeke & Luther)*

May 24—Travis T. Flory, actor *(Everybody Hates Chris)*

June 4—Earvin Johnson III, son of NBA forward Magic Johnson

June 5—Emily Seebohm, Australian swimmer

June 9—Philippe Coutinho, English musician and actor *(Waterloo Road)*

June 10—Kate Upton, model and actress

June 12—Allie DiMeco, musician and actress *(The Naked Brothers Band)*

June 12—Philippe Coutinho, Brazilian football player

June 14—Daryl Sabara, actor *(Spy Kids)*

June 23—Bridget Sloan, gymnast

July 8—Taylor Maine Pearl Brooks, daughter of country singer Garth Brooks

July 8—Benjamin Grosvenor, English classical pianist

July 10—Kristin Allen, acrobatic gymnast

July 15—Koharu Kusumi, Japanese singer and model

July 21—Rachael Flatt, figure skater

July 22—Selena Gomez, singer and actress *(Wizards of Waverly Place)*

August 2—Hallie Kate Eisenberg, actress and sister of actor Jesse Eisenberg

August 4—Tiffany Evans, singer

August 7—Bobby Bryant, boxer

August 13—Katharine Close, Scripps National Spelling Bee champion of 2006

August 18—Rebecca Brown, musician and actress *(School of Rock)*

August 20—Demi Lovato, singer *(Here We Go Again)* and actress *(Sonny With a Chance)*

August 26—Hayley Hasselhoff, actress and daughter of actor David Hasselhoff

August 26—Yang Yilin, Chinese gymnast

August 31—Holly Earl, English actress *(Doctor Who: The Doctor, the Widow, and the Wardrobe)*

September 9—Damian McGinty, Irish singer and actor *(The Glee Project)*

September 16—Nick Jonas, singer and actor, member of The Jonas Brothers

September 27—Jake Burbage, actor *(Grounded for Life)*

September 28—Keir Gilchrist, English actor *(United States of Tara)*

September 29—Marina Antipova, Russian ice dancer

September 30—Marina Windsor, granddaughter of English prince Edward, Duke of Kent

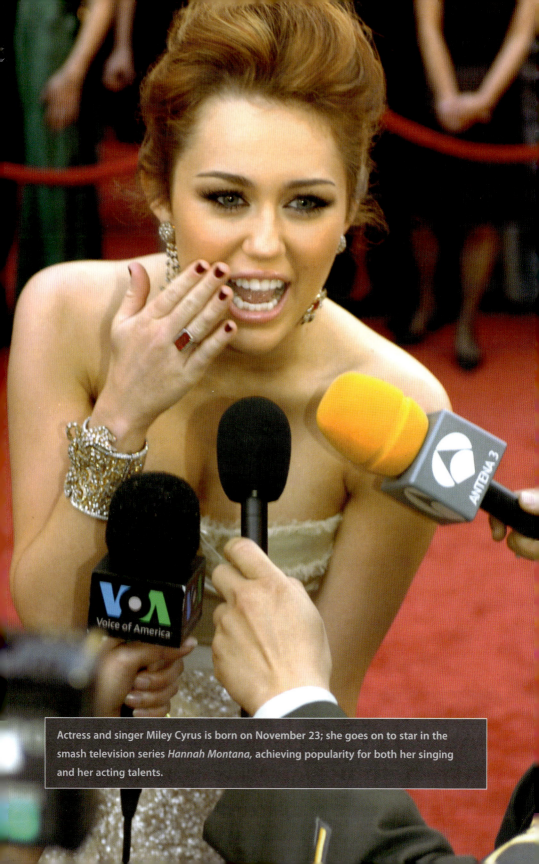

Actress and singer Miley Cyrus is born on November 23; she goes on to star in the smash television series *Hannah Montana,* achieving popularity for both her singing and her acting talents.

October 6—Rhyon Nicole Brown, actress, singer, and dancer

October 9—Tyler James Williams, actor *(Everybody Hates Chris)*

October 11—Sarah Cannon, daughter of Christian singer-songwriter Amy Grant

October 12—Josh Hutcherson, actor *(The Hunger Games)*

October 12—Taylor Horn, singer-songwriter and actress

October 16—Bryce Harper, baseball outfielder (Washington Nationals)

October 17—Sam Concepcion, Filipino singer, dancer, actor, and model

October 22—Sofia Vassilieva, actress *(My Sister's Keeper)*

October 28—Jermaine Crawford, actor *(The Wire)*

October 30—Tequan Richmond, a.k.a. T-Rich, rapper and actor *(Everybody Hates Chris)*

November 11—Trey Smith (b. Willard Christopher Smith III), actor and son of actor Will Smith

November 17—Darian Weiss, model and actor *(Better Luck Tomorrow)*

November 18—Nathan Kress, actor *(iCarly)*

November 23—Miley Cyrus, actress *(Hannah Montana)* and singer *(Can't Be Tamed)*, and daughter of country singer Billy Ray Cyrus

November 25—Ana Bogdan, Romanian tennis player

November 26—Louis Ducruet, son of Princess Stéphanie of Monaco and Daniel Ducruet

December 3—Joseph McManners, English singer-songwriter *(In Dreams)* and actor

December 8—Katie Stevens, singer and *American Idol* contestant

December 17—Thomas Law, British actor *(EastEnders)*

December 17—Jordan Garrett, actor *(Death Sentence)*

December 23—Spencer Daniels, television and film actor *(Star Trek [2009])*

December 24—Melissa Suffield, British actress *(EastEnders)*

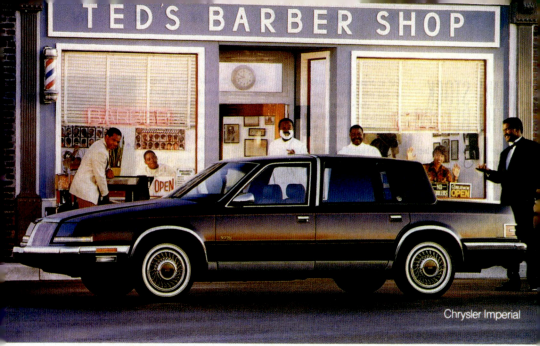

Chrysler Imperial

It Will Do All Your Talking For You.

You don't have to say a thing. Because you're driving the 1992 Chrysler Imperial.

You don't have to breathe a word about the available luxury Mark Cross™ leather seats with vinyl trim you've chosen to enhance your driving pleasure.

And of course you don't need to mention the optional hands-free visorphone that lets you keep your hands on the wheel and your eyes on the road.

And your lips are sealed when it comes to the automatic load leveling suspension, standard driver's side airbag* and its powerful 3.8-liter V-6 engine. The Chrysler Imperial also comes with the Crystal Key Warranty, bumper-to-bumper protection for five years or 50,000 miles.**

So while everybody else is sounding off, you can afford to play the strong, silent type. Because all you've got to say you've already said when you said "yes" to buying or leasing your 1992 Chrysler Imperial. For free information call 1-800-4-A-CHRYSLER.

OFFICIAL SPONSOR OF THE 1992 U S A
U.S. OLYMPIC TEAM 36 USC 380   BUCKLE UP FOR SAFETY.

*Provides added safety only when seat belt is worn.
**See limited warranties, restrictions and details at dealer.
Excludes normal maintenance, adjustments and wear items.

ADVANTAGE: CHRYSLER

The **Cost** of **Living** in
1992

Looking back at the cost of common goods in the year 1992, it's remarkable that, although many things were cheaper than they are today, others were actually much more expensive than in the present. An evening at the movies in 1992 was a heck of a lot more reasonable, what with a ticket costing an average of just over $4, and gasoline to get there costing the equivalent of less than $2 in current money. But if we wanted to make our own movies, we'd have to shell out a whopping $744.99 for a Sony camcorder—and to add insult to injury, that technology would soon be replaced by digital cameras anyway. Likewise, in 1992 a videocassette recorder to preserve our favorite TV shows was still a luxury item at well over $300, but less than 20 years later the VCR would have gone from ubiquitous to dirt cheap and, finally, to virtually obsolete, thanks to such newly indispensable innovations as the DVR and streaming video content. The personal computer, now almost taken for granted, in 1992 was still a major investment. Although we may tend to wax nostalgic about the low prices in the good old days, it's evident that technological innovations start out expensive and actually become cheaper as time passes and as the technology becomes common.

The prices of other goods, meanwhile, have become almost irrelevant: although the cost to mail a letter is considerably more than 29 cents, email has drastically reduced the number of physical letters we send the old-fashioned way. These facts about what we were buying in 1992 are a vivid reminder of how much our lives and needs have changed since then.

CNG

**STOP ENGINE
NO SMOKING
FLAMMABLE GAS**

In response to the escalating price of gasoline, Congress passes the Energy Policy Act of 1992 (EPACT), which requires the federal government to start acquiring more alternative fuels vehicles. Here, a navy soldier fills up on Compressed Natural Gas, one such alternative fuel type.

Statistics about American life in 1992:

Population: 254,994,517

Year-end close of the Dow Jones Industrial Average: 3,301

Consumer Price Index: 140.3

Minimum wage: $4.25 per hour

Average income per year: $22,935

Median family income: $30,636

Average cost of a new house: $121,500, the equivalent of $189,484 in 2012

Average monthly rent: $519

Groceries:

Loaf of white bread: 75 cents

Pound of coffee: $2.39, compared to $9.99 in 2012

Dozen eggs: 89 cents

Pound of grapes: 93 cents

12-pack of Coca-Cola: $3.49

18-oz. box of Kellogg's Corn Flakes: $1.99

Gallon of milk: $2.14

Pound of bacon: $1.92

1-oz. Hershey bar: 50 cents

20-oz. box of Oreo cookies: $1.99

Chicken: 93 cents per pound

Large pizza: $9.50

Products:

Pair of nylons: $1.00

100-count aspirin: $3.84

Postage for one letter: 29 cents

Queen-sized Serta mattress set: $173.98

.75-carat diamond engagement ring: $3,290.00

Men's sweater: $19.99

Men's jeans: $23.99

Pack of cigarettes: $1.79

Ounce of gold: $344.97, compared with $1,771.36 in 2012

Appliances:

Kenmore canister vacuum cleaner: $249.99

Singer sewing machine: $269.99

Kenmore microwave: $169.99

Kenmore side-by-side refrigerator/freezer: $999.99

Gas stove: $509.99

Barry Bonds earns a Major League Baseball record $4.7 million in salary for 1992, a year in which he wins the Most Valuable Player award. This image is from the following season.

Electronics:
27" Zenith television: $739.99
Sony videocassette recorder (VCR): $344.99
Compaq Deskpro personal computer (PC): $11,299
Sony 8 mm camcorder: $744.99
Nintendo Gameboy: $89.95

Toys:
Barbie Dream House: $169.99
Magna Doodle Deluxe set: $29.99
Large (425-piece) Lego bucket: $21.99
Rock 'Em Sock 'Em Robots: $22.99
Men's Variflex Inline Skates: $59.99

Transportation:
Bus fare, New York City: $1.25
Number of new passenger cars sold: 8,213,000
Gallon of gas: $1.13, the equivalent of $1.76 in 2010 dollars
Average cost of a new car: $16,950, compared to more than $30,000 in 2011

Car and Driver's "10 Best Cars" (base price):
BMW 325i: $28,365
Cadillac Seville Touring Sedan: $39,433
Mitsubishi Eclipse AWD Turbo: $19,217
Ford Taurus SHO: $24,262
Honda Prelude Si: $19,540
Lexus SC400: $38,690
Mazda Miata: $14,650
Nissan 300ZX Turbo: $36,809
Nissan Sentra SE-R: $12,150
Toyota Camry V6: $17,103

Sports and entertainment:
Average movie ticket price: $4.15, compared to $7.89 in 2010
Adult ticket to Disneyland: $27.50, compared to $80 in 2012
Average salary of a Major League Baseball player: $1,084,408
Salary of National League Most Valuable Player Barry Bonds: $4.7 million
    (a record at the time)
Cost of a TV commercial aired during the Super Bowl: $850,000

With a message that appeals to American youth, including an appearance on TV playing the saxophone, William Jefferson Clinton is elected our 42nd president on November 3, 1992.

Day-by-Day Calendar of 1992

T he year 1992 was a tumultuous one, marked by dramatic events both good and bad. In this year of the presidential election, the nation watched what came down to a race between incumbent Republican president George H.W. Bush and Democratic candidate Bill Clinton—with some comic relief offered by on-again-off-again candidate Ross Perot. There was nothing comic, however, about the response to the acquittal of four police officers for beating African American motorist Rodney King: the verdict touched off days of rioting in Los Angeles, California, that left 53 dead.

On the international scene, England's royal family faced its "annus horribilis," or year of disasters, with scandals breaking in the media and fire breaking out in Windsor Castle. Violence in Somalia and Bosnia led America to join the world in attempting to improve conditions, and concerns over Iraq's failure to comply with disarmament demands created tension at home.

But Americans had plenty of entertainment to hold their attention as well. The Olympic games were broadcast from Albertville, France, and Barcelona, Spain. The shakeup of late-night talk-show hosts in the wake of Johnny Carson's departure from the *Tonight Show* was as dramatic as any scripted television. Whitney Houston captivated the country with her romantic movie *The Bodyguard* and its theme song, "I Will Always Love You," which—though written by country-music legend Dolly Parton— became Houston's signature tune. Jack Palance introduced one-armed pushups to the Oscars, and Dan Quayle introduced a new spelling of *potato* to the nation's schoolchildren. It was a year of laughter and fear, sadness and triumph, and a year we'll never forget.

JANUARY 1

The United Nations declares 1992 International Space Year.

JANUARY 2

Australian cricketer Shane Warne, who would win acclaim as a bowler, plays his first test match.

JANUARY 3

Thirty-two Cubans defect to the United States via helicopter.

JANUARY 4

Michael Jackson's "Black or White" is number one on *Billboard*'s Hot 100 list.

JANUARY 5

John Guare's award-winning play *Six Degrees of Separation* closes in New York after a run of 496 performances. The following year would see a film adaptation starring Will Smith.

JANUARY 6

Robert Schenkkan's *Kentucky Cycle* premieres in Los Angeles, California. It would win the Pulitzer Prize for Drama this year.

JANUARY 7

AT&T releases the first video telephone to the public for $1,499.

JANUARY 8

At a state dinner in Japan, President Bush falls ill and vomits into the lap of Prime Minister Kiichi Miyazawa. The mishap is caught on television.

JANUARY 9

Bosnian Serbs declare an independent republic within Bosnia and Herzegovina.

JANUARY 10

The eighth annual Soap Opera Digest Awards are given.

JANUARY 11

Musician Paul Simon begins a tour in South Africa, the first major artist to tour there since the cultural boycott.

JANUARY 12

A new constitution is approved in Mali, allowing citizens to form political parties.

JANUARY 13

The trial of serial killer Jeffrey Dahmer begins. He pleads guilty but insane.

JANUARY 14

Time magazine's cover story assesses the severity of the recession.

JANUARY 15

Slovenia and Croatia gain independence from Yugoslavia.

JANUARY 16

El Salvador officials and rebel leaders end the country's 12-year civil war.

JANUARY 17

The *Boston Globe* reports that most White House employees drive foreign cars rather than supporting American auto makers.

JANUARY 18

The 49th Golden Globe Awards are broadcast. Disney's animated musical *Beauty and the Beast* and crime drama *Bugsy* win Best Picture in their respective categories.

The ninth generation of Ford's long-running F-150 series of trucks is released. Among other changes, the "Flareside" styling is brought back, having been dropped in 1988.

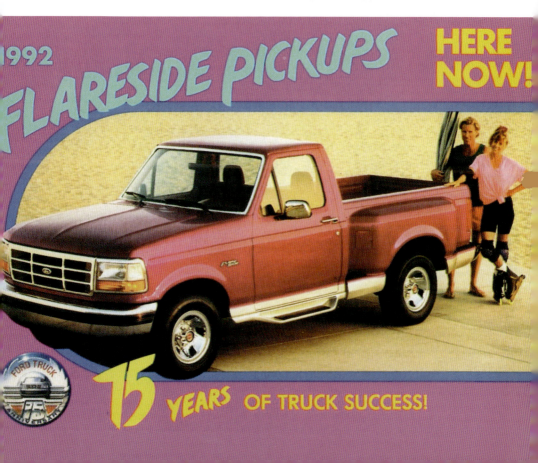

JANUARY 19

Shawn Johnson, an American gymnast who would go on to win the all-around silver medal in the 2008 Olympics, is born.

JANUARY 20

Time magazine's cover story asks, "Why Are Men and Women Different?"

JANUARY 21

The Food and Drug Administration orders Dow to release information about the silicone breast implants it manufactures.

JANUARY 22

According to the *London Daily Star,* English princess Sarah Ferguson wears a paper bag over her head during an airplane trip and pelts fellow passengers with sugar packets.

JANUARY 23

The UN Security Council commands Libya to release two men suspected in the 1988 bombing of Pan Am flight 103, which went down over Lockerbie, Scotland, claiming 270 lives.

JANUARY 24

"All 4 Love" by Color Me Badd claims the top position on the *Billboard* Hot 100 list.

JANUARY 25

American speed skater Dan Jansen skates the 500-meter in 36.41 seconds, a world record.

JANUARY 26

The Americans with Disabilities Act goes into effect.

JANUARY 27

Gennifer Flowers alleges that she and presidential candidate Bill Clinton had a 12-year-long affair.

JANUARY 28

Bill Clinton makes the cover of *Time* magazine.

JANUARY 29

Independent filmmaker Michael Mfume's debut movie, *The Weekend It Lives,* premiers in Baltimore, Maryland, to a deafening lack of applause.

JANUARY 30

Space shuttle STS-42 *(Discovery)* lands at Edwards Air Force Base, California.

JANUARY 31

Sportscaster Howard Cosell retires. The brash former lawyer, whose catchphrase was "I'm just telling it like it is," had been hugely influential in sports journalism.

FEBRUARY 1

President George H.W. Bush and Boris Yeltsin proclaim a formal end to the Cold War.

FEBRUARY 2

The Internal Revenue Service and country music singer-songwriter Willie Nelson come to a negotiated total for the music star's unpaid taxes owed: $9 million (reduced from $16.7 million).

FEBRUARY 3

Time magazine's cover story presents, in the words of the headline, "a scorching look at political correctness, social breakdown, and the culture of complaint."

FEBRUARY 4

Hugo Chávez unsuccessfully attempts a coup d'état against the Venezuelan government of Carlos Andrés Pérez.

Murphy Brown wins its second Emmy for Outstanding Comedy Series in 1992, but also causes a controversy when Vice President Dan Quayle criticizes the title character, played by Candice Bergen (shown here with Joe Regalbuto following the 1989 Emmy Awards), for becoming a single mother.

FEBRUARY 5

Jury selection begins in Los Angeles in the trial of the four police officers accused of brutality toward African-American motorist Rodney King.

FEBRUARY 6

NBC airs a 10th-anniversary special episode of *Late Night With David Letterman,* broadcast from Radio City Music Hall.

FEBRUARY 7

The European Union is formed with the signing of the Maastricht Treaty.

FEBRUARY 8

The opening ceremony for the 1992 Winter Olympics is held in Albertville, France.

FEBRUARY 9

The 42nd NBA All-Star game is held in Orlando, Florida.
Led by Magic Johnson, the West beats the East 153–113.

FEBRUARY 10

Writer Alex Haley, author of *Roots* and *The Autobiography of Malcolm X,* dies at age 70.

FEBRUARY 11

American runner Michael Johnson sets a world record for the indoor 400-meter, 44.97 seconds.

FEBRUARY 12

"I'm Too Sexy" by the English trio Right Said Fred is at number one on the *Billboard* Hot 100.

FEBRUARY 13

Major League Baseball's José Canseco is charged with ramming his wife's BMW with his Porsche.

FEBRUARY 14

A Somalian cease-fire begins.

FEBRUARY 15

Serial killer Jeffrey Dahmer is found sane and guilty of killing 15 boys.

FEBRUARY 16

The Los Angeles Lakers retire Magic Johnson's jersey number, 32.

FEBRUARY 17

Dahmer is sentenced to life in prison.

FEBRUARY 18

In the ongoing Iraq disarmament crisis, a special report of the executive chairman of UNSCOM reveals that Iraq is refusing to abide by the disarmament resolutions.

FEBRUARY 19

Crazy for You, "The New Gershwin Musical Comedy," based on George and Ira Gershwin's 1930 musical *Girl Crazy,* opens at the Shubert Theatre. It would win that year's Tony Award.

FEBRUARY 20

Texas billionaire H. Ross Perot declares his
intention to run for president on *Larry King Live.*

FEBRUARY 21

American Kristi Yamaguchi wins the Olympic
gold medal in women's figure skating.

Nirvana's *Nevermind* reaches number one on the U.S. *Billboard* Top 200 chart, heralding the
emergence of the grunge music style that dominates much of the 1990s.

FEBRUARY 22

Kurt Cobain of influential grunge band Nirvana marries Courtney Love.

FEBRUARY 23

The Winter Olympic Games close in Albertville, France.

FEBRUARY 24

Time magazine's cover story is "Holy Alliance: How Reagan and the Pope Conspired to Assist Poland's Solidarity Movement and Hasten the Demise of Communism."

FEBRUARY 25

The 34th Grammy Awards are broadcast; a new version of "Unforgettable" in which Natalie Cole accompanies her late father, Nat King Cole, wins Song of the Year.

FEBRUARY 26

Howard Korder's play *Search and Destroy* opens at the Circle in the Square Theater in New York. It would run for only 46 performances.

FEBRUARY 27

At age 16, Tiger Woods becomes the youngest PGA golfer in 35 years.

FEBRUARY 28

The Associated Press reports the death of Marguerite
Ross Barnett, president of the University of Houston, the
first black woman to be head of a major American university.

FEBRUARY 29

Canadian golfer Dawn Coe-Jones wins the Women's Kemper Open.

MARCH 1

American Jenny Thompson swims the 100-meter
freestyle in a world record 1 minute, 1.4 seconds.

MARCH 2

Sixteen-year-old American athlete Anita Nall takes three medals—gold,
silver, and bronze—in Olympic women's swimming competitions. Earlier
in the year she had set a world record time for the 200-meter breaststroke.

MARCH 3

President Bush apologizes for raising taxes after having pledged not to.

MARCH 4

The *Billboard* Hot 100 is topped by "To Be With You" by hard rock band Mr. Big.

MARCH 5

NASA announces that a new method of growing bone cells will be tested in zero gravity on the next space shuttle mission. The experiment is a joint project of NASA and the Walter Reed Army Institute of Research in Washington, D.C.

MARCH 6

The Michelangelo Virus is activated on personal computers.

MARCH 7

The so-called Wolfowitz Doctrine, which was never intended for public release, is leaked to the *New York Times*. Authored by U.S. undersecretary of defense for policy Paul Wolfowitz and his deputy, Scooter Libby, the document outlines U.S. foreign and defense policies, which are deemed imperialistic by readers. The controversy forces a revision, helmed by Dick Cheney and Colin Powell.

MARCH 8

Baseball's Mark McGwire opens up to reporter Pedro Gomez
about the emotional turmoil that caused his 1991 slump.

President George Bush hosts USSR leader Boris Yeltsin for a summit meeting in July to
discuss nuclear arms reductions. With the agreement to no longer target each other's cities
with their nuclear armaments, this summit serves as the basis for the START II treaty, signed
in 1993, and advances the end of the Cold War.

MARCH 9

Feminists Susan Faludi and Gloria Steinem are featured on the cover of *Time* magazine.

MARCH 10

On "Super Tuesday," President Bush and Arkansas governor Bill Clinton win most of the primary elections held.

MARCH 11

Irish rock band U2 receives glowing reviews for the previous night's Zoo TV Tour performance in Philadelphia. It had been five years since they last toured America.

MARCH 12

Mauritius, off the coast of Africa, becomes a republic. It had gained its independence from British rule on the same month and day in 1968.

MARCH 13

An earthquake registering 6.8 on the Richter scale kills more than 500 people in eastern Turkey.

MARCH 14

The benefit concert Farm Aid V takes place in Irving, Texas. The performers include Willie Nelson, Arlo Guthrie, John Mellencamp, and Bonnie Raitt.

MARCH 15

The United Nations expands its peacekeeping forces to unprecedented levels; their efforts for this year are estimated to cost $1 billion.

MARCH 16

Talk-show host Jay Leno, chosen to succeed Johnny Carson on the *Tonight Show*, is depicted in an Al Hirschfeld caricature on the cover of *Time* magazine.

MARCH 17

The 18th People's Choice Awards are hosted by singer Kenny Rogers. Among the winners are *Home Improvement,* voted Favorite New TV Comedy, and *City Slickers,* which wins Favorite Comedy Motion Picture.

MARCH 18

White South Africans vote in favor of political reforms, ending the apartheid regime and creating a multiracial government.

MARCH 19

Prince Andrew of England and his wife, the former
Sarah Ferguson, announce their separation.

MARCH 20

The provocative thriller *Basic Instinct,* starring Michael Douglas
and Sharon Stone, is released in the United States.

MARCH 21

Vanessa Williams's ballad "Save the Best for Last" begins
its five-week reign at the top of the *Billboard* Hot 100.

MARCH 22

US Air flight 405 from New York to Cleveland
crashes at takeoff from LaGuardia, killing 27.

MARCH 23

The Florida Marlins baseball team (now
the Miami Marlins) begins selling tickets.

MARCH 24

Space shuttle *Atlantis 11* launches, carrying
the first Belgian in space, Dirk Frimout.

MARCH 25

Cosmonaut Sergei Krikalev returns to Earth after
a 10-month stay aboard the Mir space station.

Alex Haley, author of *Roots: The Saga of an American Family* and co-author of
The Autobiography of Malcolm X, passes away on February 10. The *Roots* television
miniseries adaptation was a national sensation. Haley Heritage Park, in Knoxville,
Tennessee, is shown.

MARCH 26

Boxer Mike Tyson is sentenced to 10 years
in prison for the rape of Desiree Washington.

MARCH 27

Microsoft releases Microsoft Excel 4.0 for Windows.

MARCH 28

Winners in the American Comedy Awards include Billy Crystal,
Tracey Ullman, Bill Engvall, Lily Tomlin, and Jack Palance.

MARCH 29

The 12th Golden Raspberry Awards are announced;
Bruce Willis's film *Hudson Hawk* wins Worst Picture.

MARCH 30

Billy Crystal hosts the 64th Academy Awards. The telecast is livened by banter
between Crystal and his *City Slickers* costar, Jack Palance, who achieves instant
notoriety by doing one-handed pushups when accepting his Oscar for Best
Supporting Actor. Crystal would win an Emmy for this hosting appearance.

MARCH 31

The UN Security Council vote to ban flights and arm sales to Libya.

APRIL 1

The battleship USS *Missouri,* on which Japan surrendered, ending World War II, is decommissioned.

APRIL 2

Mafia boss John Gotti is convicted of the murder of mob boss Paul Castellano and of racketeering.

APRIL 3

Woody Harrelson, Bill Murray, and Axl Rose of Guns N' Roses are among the celebrities making the news in today's issue of *Entertainment Weekly.*

APRIL 4

New Age composer and television personality John Tesh marries actress Connie Selleca.

APRIL 5

Bosnia and Herzegovina (minus the Serbian delegation) proclaims independence from Yugoslavia. Serbian troops besiege the city of Sarajevo.

APRIL 6

Isaac Asimov, science fiction author and one of the most prolific writers of all time, dies from infections related to HIV transmitted to him from a blood transfusion.

APRIL 7

America recognizes the independence of what is now known as *Republika Srpska,* one of two entities comprising Bosnia and Herzegovina.

APRIL 8

The final issue of Britain's humorous and satirical *Punch Magazine* is released. Founded in 1841, the magazine had published works by such famous writers as Charles Dickens and William Makepeace Thackeray, and shaped the concept of the modern cartoon.

APRIL 9

William O. Studeman becomes deputy director of the CIA.

APRIL 10

The National Hockey League players' strike ends after 10 days.

Kristi Yamaguchi wins the gold medal in Women's Figure Skating at the 1992 Winter Olympics on February 21, the first person of Asian descent to medal in that event.

APRIL 11

The Cleveland Indians set a team record for long game loss to the Boston Red Sox: 19 innings, lasting 6.5 hours.

APRIL 12

Euro Disneyland (now Disneyland Paris) opens.

APRIL 13

The Chicago Flood occurs when the damaged wall of a utility tunnel beneath the Chicago River opens, flooding basements and underground facilities throughout the Chicago Loop.

APRIL 14

Guys & Dolls opens at Martin Beck Theater in New York, where it would run for 1,143 performances and win the Tony Award for Best Revival.

APRIL 15

On this tax day, billionairess Leona Helmsley, the "Queen of Mean," reports to prison to begin serving time for tax evasion.

APRIL 16

The tanker *Katina P.* runs aground off of Maputo, Mozambique, spilling 60,000 tons of crude oil into the ocean.

APRIL 17

Democratic presidential candidate Jerry Brown states that his campaign slogan, "We the People," is not a reference to the slogan "We Are the People," used by the presidential candidate in Martin Scorsese's 1976 film *Taxi Driver*.

APRIL 18

Comedian Jerry Seinfeld hosts perennial sketch-comedy show *Saturday Night Live*. The musical guest is Annie Lennox, formerly of the Eurythmics.

APRIL 19

The top three *New York Times* bestselling books in paperback are John Grisham's *The Firm*, Fannie Flagg's *Fried Green Tomatoes at the Whistle Stop Café*, and Pat Conroy's *The Prince of Tides*.

APRIL 20

The Freddie Mercury Tribute Concert in London raises millions of dollars for AIDS research. Held at Wembley Stadium, the event is broadcast to more than one billion television viewers. Queen frontman Mercury had died the previous November.

APRIL 21

Murderer Robert Alton Harris is executed by gas chamber in San Quentin State Prison. This is California's first execution since 1967.

APRIL 22

A 6.1-magnitude earthquake strikes Joshua Tree, California.

APRIL 23

McDonald's opens its first fast-food restaurant in China.

APRIL 24

English musician and actor David Bowie marries Somali-born supermodel Iman in Switzerland.

APRIL 25

In the Firestone World Bowling Tournament of Champions, Marc McDowell defeats Don Genalo 223–193.

APRIL 26

Author Alex Haley *(Roots)* wins the 1992 Ellis Island Award posthumously.

A scandal over 1990 Grammy award–winning recordings by Milli Vanilli, which were lip-synched instead of actually sung by the performers, is resolved on March 24, when a judge rules that consumers can get a $3 refund if they can prove they bought a Milli Vanilli album prior to November 27, 1990.

APRIL 27

Betty Boothroyd becomes the first female
Speaker of the British House of Commons.

APRIL 28

Serbia and Montenegro form the Federal Republic of Yugoslavia.

APRIL 29

Six days of riots begin in Los Angeles following the acquittal of the four police
officers tried for beating Rodney King. The rioting would spread as far as Atlanta,
Georgia. In Los Angeles, the violence would leave 53 dead and thousands injured.

APRIL 30

The final episode of *The Cosby Show* airs on NBC. The sitcom had aired
for eight seasons. Its spinoff, *A Different World,* would air for six seasons.

MAY 1

Former Lindhurst student Eric Houston kills four and wounds nine
in a shooting at Lindhurst High School in Olivehurst, California.

MAY 2

The 118th Kentucky Derby is held; Pat Day aboard
Lil E. Tee wins in 2 minutes, 3 seconds.

MAY 3

"Jump" by Atlanta rap duo Kriss Kross reigns at the number
one spot on the *Billboard* Hot 100, where it would stay
for eight weeks. The single would go double platinum.

MAY 4

At Kent State University, where in 1970 unarmed students were fatally
shot by Ohio National Guardsmen, controversial civil rights activist William
Kunstler delivers a speech recalling the tragic events of 22 years earlier.

MAY 5

Country singer Tammy Wynette is hospitalized with an
infection. Earlier this year, future First Lady Hillary Clinton
had displeased the country legend by making a disparaging
reference to her classic song "Stand by Your Man"
in the context of Clinton's career as distinct from
that of her husband, Bill. Clinton later apologized.

MAY 6

German-born actress and singer Marlene Dietrich dies, age 90. Originally brought to Hollywood to be Paramount Studios' rival to MGM screen siren Greta Garbo, Dietrich became an icon in her own right, appearing in such films as *The Blue Angel, Witness for the Prosecution, Destry Rides Again,* and Alfred Hitchcock's *Stage Fright.*

MAY 7

Space shuttle *Endeavor* makes its maiden flight.

MAY 8

The first issue of street newspaper *Spare Change News* appears. The publication is produced by the Homeless Empowerment Project, located in Cambridge, Massachusetts.

MAY 9

Nineteen-year-old Michelle McLean of Namibia is crowned the 41st Miss Universe.

MAY 10

The Bible Lands Museum opens in Jerusalem.

MAY 11

Time magazine's cover story is on the Rodney King riots.

A child prodigy, seven-time U.S. Chess Champion, and perennial World Chess Championship contender, Samuel Reshevsky passes away on April 4 at the age of 81.

MAY 12

Mount Everest marks two firsts: the first Belgian woman to reach the summit, Ingrid Baeyens, and the first Israeli to do so, Doron Erel.

MAY 13

The final episode of *Night Court* airs on NBC. The sitcom had first aired in January of 1984, and over the years the cast had included Harry Anderson, John Larroquette, Markie Post, and Marsha Warfield.

MAY 14

Three California schools ban hypnotists from performing at school functions.

MAY 15

The third film in the *Lethal Weapon* franchise is released. It stars Mel Gibson, Danny Glover, Joe Pesci, and Rene Russo.

MAY 16

Weird Al Yankovic's "Smells Like Nirvana," a parody of grunge group Nirvana's hit "Smells Like Teen Spirit," hits number 35 on the *Billboa14rd* Hot 100.

MAY 17

The entertainment world loses two prominent figures: Lawrence Welk, former bandleader and television host, who dies at the age of 89; and Hollywood photographer George Hurrell, whose publicity portraits of stars like Norma Shearer, Joan Crawford, and Errol Flynn helped shape their glamorous image. Hurrell was 87.

MAY 18

The Supreme Court rules that states cannot force mentally unstable criminal defendants to take antipsychotic drugs.

MAY 19

The 27th amendment to the Constitution is officially certified, 202 years after it was first proposed. Members of Congress can no longer give themselves mid-session raises.

MAY 20

India launches its first satellite.

MAY 21

The People's Republic of China conducts a nuclear weapons test at the Lop Nor Base.

MAY 22

Johnny Carson hosts the
Tonight Show for the last time.

MAY 23

President Bush orders the Coast Guard to
intercept boats with Haitian refugees.

MAY 24

Al Unser Jr. wins the Indianapolis 500.

MAY 25

Jay Leno becomes the regular
host of the *Tonight Show*.

MAY 26

Charles Geschke, president of Adobe Systems, is kidnapped
from his company parking lot. He would be freed on
May 31 and his two kidnappers sentenced to life in prison.

MAY 27

Canadian-born Leneen Forde becomes the first woman governor of an Australian state when she is appointed governor of Queensland, Australia.

MAY 28

Thirteen-year-old Amanda Goad correctly spells "lyceum" and wins the 65th National Spelling Bee.

Retail shopping pioneer Sam Walton, founder of Wal-Mart and Sam's Club, passes away on April 5. *Time* magazine recognized him as one of the 100 Most Influential People of the 20th Century.

MAY 29

Sister Act, starring Whoopi Goldberg and
Maggie Smith, is released in theaters.

MAY 30

The UN votes for sanctions against
Serb-led Yugoslavia to halt fighting.

MAY 31

The 46th Tony Awards are presented; *Dancing at Lughnasa*
wins Best Play, and *Crazy for You* takes Best Musical.

JUNE 1

Kentucky celebrates its statehood bicentennial.

JUNE 2

The Maastricht Treaty is defeated in a referendum in Denmark, a move
considered to be a hitch in the progress toward European integration.

JUNE 3

The United Nations Conference on Environment and Development, or Earth Summit, opens in Rio de Janeiro, Brazil.

JUNE 4

San Jose, California, voters reject a plan to built a new football stadium.

JUNE 5

Entertainment Weekly reports that Sylvester Stallone is "buffing up" in preparation for his role in the upcoming sci-fi/action film *Demolition Man,* which would also star Wesley Snipes and Sandra Bullock.

JUNE 6

Tony Award–winning theater and film actor Ben Vereen suffers serious injuries when he is struck by a car.

JUNE 7

Emmy-nominated director, actor, and producer Bob Sweeney dies at age 73. Sweeney is best remembered for having directed the first three seasons of the *Andy Griffith Show.*

JUNE 8

New York Yankees pitcher Steve Howe is banned
from baseball for life because of drug abuse.

JUNE 9

The Houston Astros lose to the San
Diego Padres 5–4 at Jack Murphy Stadium.

JUNE 10

The notorious tabloid *Weekly World News* reports
on \melting plastic surgery, Pacific islanders who
"scamper around on three legs," and nine-foot
ants that attack jungle explorers in South America.

JUNE 11

The Seattle Mariners baseball team
is sold to Nintendo Co., a Japanese firm.

JUNE 12

Entertainment Weekly notes that the latest fitness fad, kickboxing, has been
taken up by movie stars Michelle Pfeiffer, Laura Dern, and Jodie Foster.

JUNE 13

Tyler Davison, the world's smallest baby at six inches and 11 ounces, is born.

Farmous for his science fiction series, including the Foundation series and the Robot series, iconic science fiction writer and editor Isaac Asimov dies on April 6. His image is seen here on the cover of his self-titled science fiction magazine.

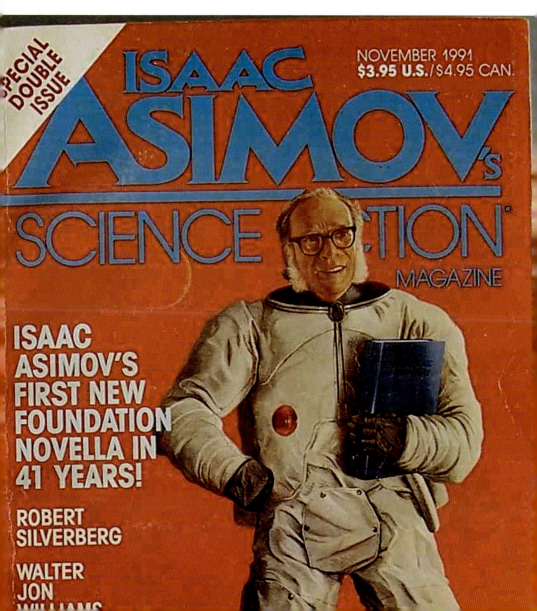

JUNE 14

Mona Van Duyn is named the United States' first female poet laureate.

JUNE 15

Working from an inaccurate flashcard, vice president Dan Quayle corrects a 12-year-old in a spelling bee, insisting that "potato" is spelled "potatoe."

JUNE 16

President Reagan's defense secretary, Caspar Weinberger, is indicted in the Iran-Contra affair.

JUNE 17

The Philadelphia 76ers trade Charles Barkley to the Phoenix Suns.

JUNE 18

The NHL draft begins.

JUNE 19

Tim Burton's film *Batman Returns* is released in the United States. It stars Michael Keaton, Michelle Pfeiffer, and Danny DeVito.

JUNE 20

"I'll Be There" by Mariah Carey begins its two-week
run as number one on the *Billboard* Hot 100.

JUNE 21

The U.S. Open concludes; Tom Kite wins with 285 strokes.

JUNE 22

President George Bush presents Microsoft chairman
Bill Gates with the National Medal of Technology.

JUNE 23

The 19th Daytime Emmy Awards are presented; actress Susan
Lucci *(All My Children)* is passed over for the 13th time.

JUNE 24

At age 43, Grammy Award–winning musician Billy Joel receives
an honorary diploma from Hicksville (New York) High School.

JUNE 25

In Istanbul, 11 countries establish the Black Sea Economic Corporation,
which is intended to foster good relations in the Black Sea area.

JUNE 26

India leases Tin Bigha corridor to
Bangladesh amid much protesting.

JUNE 27

At Wimbledon, 193rd-ranked Andrei Olhovsky
defeats number one seed Jim Courier.

JUNE 28

Two earthquakes, including the third strongest
in U.S. history (7.4 magnitude), rock California.

JUNE 29

Algerian president Mohamed Boudiaf is assassinated
during a televised speech. Bodyguard Lieutenant
Lembarek Boumaârafi would be convicted of the crime.

JUNE 30

Fidel Ramos is installed as president of the Philippines.

JULY 1

A League of Their Own, starring Tom Hanks and Geena Davis, is released in theaters. Directed by Penny Marshall, the comedy-drama takes inspiration from the actual history of the All-American Girls Professional Baseball League.

JULY 2

President Bush holds a news conference with foreign journalists. Among the topics discussed are Polish reforms and aid to Russia.

Following the April 29h acquittal of four Los Angeles police officers—three white, one Hispanic—who were videotaped beating African-American motorist Rodney King at the end of a high-speed chase, rioting breaks out in the Los Angeles area, involving thousands of people.

JULY 3

Massachusetts senator Ted Kennedy marries Victoria Reggie.

JULY 4

Musician John Phillips of the Mamas & the Papas ("California Dreamin'")
undergoes a liver transplant. Later, caught drinking alcohol
in public, he would joke that he was "breaking in" the new liver.

JULY 5

The 106th Wimbledon Men's Tennis tournament concludes with Andre
Agassi beating Goran Ivanisevic, resulting in Agassi's first Grand Slam title.

JULY 6

Sir Mix-a-Lot's tribute to callipygean women, "Baby Got Back," is number
one on the *Billboard* Hot 100. It would hold that position for five weeks.

JULY 7

Patrick Muldoon makes his debut appearance on the soap
opera *Days of Our Lives.* He would go on to appear in
Saved by the Bell, Melrose Place, and the film *Starship Troopers.*

JULY 8

The Conference for Security and Co-operation in Europe creates the office of high commissioner on national minorities.

JULY 9

Movie star Kim Basinger *(L.A. Confidential)* gets a star on the Hollywood Walk of Fame.

JULY 10

The U.S. Major Soccer League folds after 14 seasons.

JULY 11

Patricia Parker, head of the Operations Division at the Space Telescope Science Institute in Baltimore, Maryland, receives a Goddard Exceptional Achievement Award for her "outstanding leadership and management in the execution and enhancement of the science operations of the Hubble Space Telescope."

JULY 12

Rocker Axl Rose is arrested at New York's JFK airport on riot charges relating to a concert in St. Louis, Missouri, the previous year.

JULY 13

Yitzhak Rabin becomes prime minister of
Israel. He would be assassinated in 1995.

JULY 14

Computer program 386BSD is released by Lynne and William Jolitz,
beginning the Open Source Operating System Revolution.
Linus Torvalds would release Linux soon afterwards.

JULY 15

Pope John Paul II is hospitalized for three
weeks to have a tumor removed.

JULY 16

At the Democratic National Convention, Bill Clinton is officially nominated
for president, with Tennessee senator Al Gore as his running mate.

JULY 17

Amid falling poll numbers, Ross Perot drops out of the presidential race.

JULY 18

Singers Whitney Houston and Bobby Brown marry.

JULY 19

Ebony P. Warren is crowned the 24th Miss Black America.

The fifth and last completed space shuttle built, the *Endeavour* takes her maiden flight on May 7.

JULY 20

The Around the World Air Race begins when
31 planes take off from Paris, France.

JULY 21

This week's issue of *Time* magazine
profiles Bill Clinton and Al Gore.

JULY 22

Colombian drug lord Pablo
Escobar escapes from prison.

JULY 23

Bruce Springsteen *(Born in the USA)* begins a world tour.

JULY 24

Commissioner of baseball Fay Vincent reinstates New York Yankeesowner
George Steinbrenner, who had been banned from baseball two years before.

JULY 25

The opening ceremony for the Summer
Olympic Games is held in Barcelona, Spain.

JULY 26

The 47th U.S. Women's Open concludes;
Patty Sheehan wins with 280 strokes.

JULY 27

Swimmers Dimitri Lepikov, Vladimir Pychenko, Veniamin
Taianovitch, and Evgueni Sadovyi (Unified Team) set a world
record in the 4x200-meter freestyle at 7 minutes, 11.95 seconds.

JULY 28

The Florida Marlins break ground on their spring training stadium.

JULY 29

Actor Ray Sharkey (*Wiseguys*) is arrested for possession of narcotics.

JULY 30

Lin Li of China swims a world record in the women's
200-meter medley: 2 minutes, 11.65 seconds.

JULY 31

A Thai Airbus crashes into a
mountain at Katmandu, killing 113.

AUGUST 1

The Saturday edition of NBC's *Today* show premiers.
The Sunday edition had preceded it five years before.

AUGUST 2

The United States imposes a "no-fly zone" over
south Iraq and begins air patrols of the zone.

AUGUST 3

Time magazine takes a sobering look at the
ongoing struggle with the AIDS epidemic.

AUGUST 4

Ralph Cooper, creator and emcee of *Amateur Night at the Apollo,* dies. The program, which started in 1934, paved the way for such television programs as *American Idol.*

AUGUST 5

The four LAPD officers acquitted in the Rodney King brutality case are indicted on civil rights charges.

Bandleader and TV host Lawrence Welk passes away on May 17.

AUGUST 6

Senators urge President Bush to consider military intervention to halt the genocide in Yugoslavia.

AUGUST 7

Up against the Baltimore Orioles, the Cleveland Indians turn a triple play. Their next would not take place until August 27, 2007.

AUGUST 8

Actress Barbara Hershey *(Black Swan, The Portrait of a Lady)* marries artist Stephen Douglas in a small ceremony in Oxford, Connecticut. The marriage would end the following year.

AUGUST 9

The Olympic Games close in Barcelona, Spain.

AUGUST 10

NASA launches the satellite TOPEX *(Poseidon)* to map ocean surface topography.

AUGUST 11

The Mall of America, the largest shopping mall in the
United States, opens in Bloomington, Minnesota.

AUGUST 12

Canada, Mexico, and the United States announce the completion
of negotiations for the North American Free Trade Agreement.

AUGUST 13

Stock-car racer Clifford Allison, son of NASCAR champion
Bobby Allison and a member of the "Alabama Gang,"
dies in a crash at the Michigan International Speedway.

AUGUST 14

"This Used to Be My Playground" by Madonna closes
out its one week at the top of *Billboard*'s Hot 100.

AUGUST 15

Actress and singer Susan Anton *(Cannonball Run II)* marries
actor Jeff Lester. Five years later the couple would start
their own production company, Big Picture Studios.

AUGUST 16

The top three books on the *New York Times* list of bestselling fiction are *Gerald's Game* (Stephen King), *Waiting to Exhale* (Terry McMillan), and *The Pelican Brief* (John Grisham).

AUGUST 17

Time magazine features a shocking cover photograph of Muslim prisoners being held in a Serbian detention camp.

AUGUST 18

Frances Cobain, daughter of Nirvana frontman Kurt Cobain and Courtney Love, is born.

AUGUST 19

The *Los Angeles Times* reports on a new study indicating that the use of hot tubs early in pregnancy can cause birth defects.

AUGUST 20

The Republican National Convention officially renominates President George Bush and Vice President Dan Quayle. Across the pond, English rock star Sting marries actress Trudie Styler.

AUGUST 21

A firefight erupts when U.S. marshals are sent to arrest Randy Weaver at Ruby Ridge, Idaho, killing a marshal and Weaver's 14-year-old son, and beginning an 11-day stand-off at the Weavers' cabin.

AUGUST 22

In Ruby Ridge, Vicki Weaver is killed by an FBI sniper, Lon Horiuchi.

Glacier Girl, a WWII-era P-38 Lightning fighter plane abandoned for 50 years, is recovered from under 268 feet of ice in Greenland and eventually restored to flying condition.

AUGUST 23

Hurricane Andrew reaches category 5 status. It is only the third category 5 hurricane to make landfall in the United States.

AUGUST 24

Hurricane Andrew hits south Florida, killing 35. Total damages of the hurricane would be estimated at $26.5 billion.

AUGUST 25

Protestor Rosebud Denovo breaks into the residence of the chancellor of the University of California, Berkeley, and is killed by police.

AUGUST 26

The Broadway musical *Anna Karenina* opens in New York. Although both the book and the score would be nominated for Tony Awards, it receives poor reviews and would close after only 46 performances.

AUGUST 27

In what would later be considered one of the team's worst trades, the New York Mets trade pitcher David Cone to the Toronto Blue Jays for Ryan Thompson and Jeff Kent.

AUGUST 28

Auto manufacture in Southern California comes to an end with the closing of the General Motors plant in Van Nuys. The factory had been in operation for 45 years.

AUGUST 29

Mary Norton, English author of the beloved children's books about the Borrowers—miniature people who live unobserved alongside humans—dies at age 88. Among Norton's other writings were two books that formed the basis for the Disney movie *Bedknobs and Broomsticks*.

AUGUST 30

Nirvana appears at the Reading Festival in England and gives what would come to be viewed as one of the band's landmark performances. In 2009, a CD and DVD preserving this show would be released.

AUGUST 31

Woody Allen is featured on the cover of *Time* magazine following the revelation of his affair with his 21-year-old stepdaughter, Soon-Yi Farrow Previn.

SEPTEMBER 1

Lee P. Brown, New York City's first black police commissioner, steps down, citing personal reasons.

SEPTEMBER 2

An earthquake in Nicaragua kills at least 116 people; damage in Costa Rica is also reported.

SEPTEMBER 3

Actor Jerry Lewis's annual telethon raises more than $45 million for the treatment of muscular dystrophy.

SEPTEMBER 4

The documentary *Scared Silent: Ending and Exposing Child Abuse,* hosted by Oprah Winfrey, airs simultaneously on all three major television networks ABC, CBS, and NBC. This is the first time a program other than the news has been broadcast simultaneously on the three networks.

SEPTEMBER 5

Hurricane Iniki forms. This would be the strongest hurricane to strike Hawaii in recorded history.

SEPTEMBER 6

Algerian athlete Noureddine Morceli sets a new world record for the 1,500-meter run: 3 minutes, 28 seconds.

SEPTEMBER 7

Baseball commissioner Fay Vincent resigns.

After 30 years as host of the *Tonight Show,* Johnny Carson appears in his final show on May 22.

SEPTEMBER 8

Danny Tartabull of the New York Yankees drives in nine runs against the Baltimore Orioles. The Yankees win 16–4.

SEPTEMBER 9

Universal Pictures releases the film *Sneakers,* starring Robert Redford and Mary McDonnell, to theaters.

SEPTEMBER 10

Lucy in Charles Schultz's comic strip *Peanuts* raises the price at her psychiatric help booth from 5 cents to 47 cents.

SEPTEMBER 11

Hurricane Iniki hits the Hawaiian islands of Kauai and Oahu.

SEPTEMBER 12

Dr. Mae Jemison becomes the first African-American woman to travel into space, aboard the space shuttle *Endeavour*.

SEPTEMBER 13

The annual Lollapalooza music festival, which
started this year on July 18, closes.
Among those performing this year were
the Red Hot Chili Peppers, Stone Temple
Pilots, Soundgarden, and Pearl Jam.

SEPTEMBER 14

Hillary Rodham Clinton is featured on the cover
of *Time* magazine along with the provocative
question: "Is she helping or hurting her husband?"

SEPTEMBER 15

Ted Weiss, a Democratic member of the
House of Representatives from New York,
is posthumously elected to another term. Weiss
died of heart failure the day before the election.

SEPTEMBER 16

On what is dubbed Black Wednesday, the British
government has to withdraw the pound sterling
from the European Exchange Rate Mechanism.

SEPTEMBER 17

The House votes 280 to 128 to give the Federal Communications Commission control of cable TV rates.

SEPTEMBER 18

The Boyz II Men song "End of the Road" continues at number one on the *Billboard* Hot 100. Ultimately it would hold that position for a staggering 13 weeks, breaking the record previously held by Elvis Presley. It would also be listed as number 43 on the *Billboard* All-Time Top 100 list.

SEPTEMBER 19

The UN Security Council unanimously passes Resolution 777, in which it directs the Federal Republic of Yugoslavia (Serbia and Montenegro) to apply for membership in the United Nations.

SEPTEMBER 20

Leanza Cornett of Florida is crowned the 66th Miss America.

SEPTEMBER 21

Television and film actor Bill Williams (born Herman August Wilhelm Katt), who played the title character in the 1950s series *The Adventures of Kit Carson,* dies. His son, William Katt, had become an actor as well, starring in the *Greatest American Hero* series in the early 1980s.

SEPTEMBER 22

Violent storms strike the South of France, unleashing flash floods and leaving up to 34 people dead.

Jay Leno emerges victorious in the battle to replace legend Johnny Carson on the *Tonight Show;* his first episode broadcasts on May 25.

SEPTEMBER 23

Canadian Manon Rhéaume becomes the first
woman to play in an NHL exhibition game.

SEPTEMBER 24

Dave Winfield of the Toronto Blue Jays becomes the
oldest player (at 40) to drive in 100 runs in a season.

SEPTEMBER 25

Gregory Kingsley, 12, wins the right to divorce
his parents and live with his foster parents.

SEPTEMBER 26

Roseanne Barr Arnold gets a star on Hollywood's Walk of Fame.

SEPTEMBER 27

The ASPCA stops a Santeria ceremony in
the Bronx, saving 42 animals from sacrifice.

SEPTEMBER 28

Time magazine's cover story about the national economy asks, "Is there light at the end of the tunnel?"

SEPTEMBER 29

Magic Johnson announces his intention to return to basketball.

SEPTEMBER 30

The 26th annual Country Music Association Awards are presented, with Garth Brooks winning Entertainer of the Year.

OCTOBER 1

The Cartoon Network begins broadcasting.

OCTOBER 2

A riot in the Carandiru Penitentiary in Sao Paulo, Brazil, results in the Carandiru Massacre, in which 111 prisoners are killed.

OCTOBER 3

Controversy erupts when, after performing a song protesting child abuse by the Catholic Church, Irish singer Sinéad O'Connor rips up a photo of Pope John Paul II on *Saturday Night Live.*

OCTOBER 4

Mozambique's 16-year civil war concludes with the Rome General Peace Accords.

OCTOBER 5

President Bush's veto of the FCC bill is overturned.

OCTOBER 6

English actor Denholm Elliott, best known to American audiences as Marcus Brody in *Raiders of the Lost Ark* and *Indiana Jones and the Last Crusade,* dies at age 70. A Commander of the Order of the British Empire and a BAFTA winner for three consecutive years, he was said to be so adept at scene stealing that British actors would warn each other, "Never act with children, dogs, or Denholm Elliott."

OCTOBER 7

The Tampa Bay Lightning play their first NHL game.

OCTOBER 8

The Nobel Prize for literature is awarded to West Indies poet Derek Walcott.

OCTOBER 9

A meteorite is seen from Kentucky to New York before
it crashes on a Peekskill, New York, family's Chevy Malibu.

Boxer Oscar De La Hoya (right, with martial artist and stuntman Steven Ho) earned a gold medal at the 1992 Summer Olympics.

OCTOBER 10

Actors Ally Sheedy *(St. Elmo's Fire)* and David Lansbury marry.

OCTOBER 11

The first three-way presidential debate is held between Bush, Clinton, and Perot, who has returned to the presidential race.

OCTOBER 12

A 5.8 magnitude earthquake strikes Cairo, Egypt, killing at least 510.

OCTOBER 13

Children's book author and illustrator James Marshall dies at age 50 of a brain tumor. Marshall created the series *The Stupids* and in 2007 would be posthumously awarded the American Library Association's Laura Ingalls Wilder Medal for his "substantial and lasting contribution to literature for children."

OCTOBER 14

In the last game of the National League Championship Series, the Atlanta Braves defeat the Pittsburgh Pirates 3–2 to win the National League pennant.

OCTOBER 15

A New York City subway driver is convicted of
manslaughter in the death of five riders after
having fallen asleep while in control of the train.

OCTOBER 16

The original 1964 *Gilligan's Island* pilot is first aired on television.

OCTOBER 17

In the first game of the World Series, the
Toronto Blue Jays lose to the Atlanta Braves.

OCTOBER 18

A 6.6-magnitude earthquake hits Colombia, but there are no casualties.

OCTOBER 19

Time magazine's cover photo depicts the October 11 presidential debate.

OCTOBER 20

In the first World Series game to be played outside
the United States, Toronto beats the Atlanta Braves.

OCTOBER 21

Pop star Madonna's notorious coffee-table book *Sex* goes on
sale. Despite—or because of—its controversial content, its
original print run of 1.5 million copies sells out in mere days.

OCTOBER 22

Wendy Wasserstein's play *The Sisters Rosensweig* opens at
Mitzi Newhouse Theater in New York, where it would run
for 149 performances. It would go on to win the William Inge
Award for Distinguished Achievement in American Theatre.

OCTOBER 23

Emperor Akihito becomes the first
emperor of Japan to visit Chinese soil.

OCTOBER 24

Winning four of six games, the Toronto Blue Jays
become the first non-U.S. team to win the World Series.

OCTOBER 25

Lithuania holds a referendum on its first post-Soviet constitution.

OCTOBER 26

The London Ambulance Service is thrown into chaos when
a new computer system, Computer Aided Despatch, fails.

Causing more than $25 billion in damage, category 5 Hurricane Andrew makes landfall
in Florida on August 24.

OCTOBER 27

To mark the centennial of author J.R.R. Tolkien's birth,
England's Royal Mail releases a commemorative stamp booklet
in his honor. None of the stamps bear Tolkien's likeness.

OCTOBER 28

The prime time television lineup includes
Doogie Howser, M.D.; Seinfeld;
The Wonder Years; Home Improvement;
Beverly Hills, 90210; Melrose Place; In the Heat
of the Night; and *Unsolved Mysteries.*

OCTOBER 29

The guests of television hosts Regis Philbin and
Kathie Lee Gifford include the Olsen twins (Mary-Kate
and Ashley) of the sitcom *Full House,* country singer
Trisha Yearwood, and showmen Siegfried and Roy.

OCTOBER 30

Living on Earth, Public Radio International's environmental
news magazine, looks at electric cars and
the defeat of the fungus known as wheat rust.

OCTOBER 31

Pope John Paul II lifts the edict of the Inquisition
against Galileo Galilei and apologizes.

NOVEMBER 1

The New York City Marathon is won by Willie
Mtolo in 2 hours, 9 minutes, 29 seconds.

NOVEMBER 2

Airbus runs the first test flight of the A330.

NOVEMBER 3

Bill Clinton is elected 42nd president of the United States.

NOVEMBER 4

Released almost a month before, Steven Seagal's action flick
Under Siege is still number one in movie theaters. Also starring
Tommy Lee Jones, the film would garner two Academy Award
nominations, for Best Sound Effects Editing and Best Sound.

NOVEMBER 5

Bobby Fischer beats Boris Spassky again in a rematch in Belgrade to win the chess title, 20 years after their first game.

NOVEMBER 6

Making the news in *Entertainment Weekly* are Robin Williams, John Malkovich, and Black Crowes frontman Chris Robinson, who suggested that a less-than-ardent concertgoer "go home and watch VH-1." Ouch!

NOVEMBER 7

Film and television actor Jack Kelly dies, age 65. Kelly was best known for playing Bart Maverick in the *Maverick* TV series that ran from 1957 to 1962. Kelly later went into politics and was mayor of Huntington Beach, California, from 1983 to 1986.

NOVEMBER 8

A crowd of 300,000 demonstrates against racism in Berlin.

NOVEMBER 9

Time magazine's cover story asks, "Can GM Survive in Today's World?"

NOVEMBER 10

Kevin Joseph "Chuck" Connors dies, age 71. Well known to television audiences from the series *The Rifleman,* Connors embarked on a long and successful acting career after having already been a professional basketball and baseball player, and one of only 12 athletes to have played for both Major League Baseball and the National Basketball Association.

Forever linked to his role in Alfred Hitchcock's classic film *Psycho,* actor Anthony Perkins (here shown with Charmian Carr) passes away on September 12.

NOVEMBER 11

The Church of England votes to
allow women to become priests.

NOVEMBER 12

New York Yankees pitcher Steve Howe is
reinstated to baseball after his June ban.

NOVEMBER 13

Bram Stoker's Dracula, directed by Francis Ford Coppola,
is released in American theaters. Starring Gary Oldman,
Winona Ryder, Anthony Hopkins, and Keanu Reeves,
it would win Academy Awards for Best Costume
Design, Best Sound Effects Editing, and Best Makeup.

NOVEMBER 14

"How Do You Talk to an Angel," the theme
song from TV's *The Heights,* bumps Boyz II Men's
"End of the Road" out of the number one spot on the
Billboard Hot 100. The series would be canceled
shortly after the song fell from this pinnacle.

NOVEMBER 15

The television miniseries *The Jacksons: An American Dream* begins its run on ABC. Based on Katherine Jackson's autobiography *My Family,* it portrays the show-business success of the Jackson 5 and Michael Jackson's rise to fame as a solo artist.

NOVEMBER 16

Time magazine features on its cover president-elect Bill Clinton.

NOVEMBER 17

Dateline NBC airs a demonstration showing General Motors trucks blowing up on impact; later it is revealed that NBC rigged the test.

NOVEMBER 18

Malcolm X, starring Denzel Washington and Angela Bassett, premieres in the United States. Directed by Spike Lee, it would be film critic Roger Ebert's pick for best movie of 1992.

NOVEMBER 19

The American Cancer Society holds its
annual Great American Smokeout.

NOVEMBER 20

Windsor Castle, one of England's royal
residences, catches fire, resulting in more
than 50 million pounds' worth of damage.

NOVEMBER 21

Actor Sterling Holloway dies at age 87.
Although he had appeared in 150
movies and television shows,
he was probably best known as
the voice of Winnie the Pooh
in the Disney animated films.

NOVEMBER 22

The *Washington Post* reports that Oregon senator
Bob Packwood sexually harassed 10 women.

NOVEMBER 23

The 10 millionth cellular telephone is sold.

On September 12, Dr. Mae Jemison becomes the first African-American woman in space when she takes off as part of the crew on the space shuttle *Endeavour*.

NOVEMBER 24

On the 40th anniversary of her accession to the English throne,
Queen Elizabeth II makes a speech in which she calls 1992 an "annus horribilis"
(disastrous year), in reference to the Windsor Castle fire, the divorce of her
daughter, the publication of the tell-all book *Diana: Her True Story,* and the
separation of her son Andrew from his wife, the former Sarah Ferguson.

NOVEMBER 25

The Czechoslovakian Federal Assembly votes to split the country
into the Czech Republic and Slovakia as of January 1, 1993.

NOVEMBER 26

A Boeing 734 crashes into a mountain in China, killing 141.

NOVEMBER 27

A fire destroys the Redouten Wing of
the Hofburg Palace in Vienna, Austria.

NOVEMBER 28

Whitney Houston's hit version of the Dolly Parton song "I Will Always
Love You" begins 13 weeks as the number one single in America.

NOVEMBER 29

Italian fashion designer Emilio Pucci dies at age 78. Pucci's clients had included Sophia Loren, Jackie Kennedy, and Braniff Airlines, for whom he designed new uniforms to give the flight attendants and crew a more up-to-date look.

NOVEMBER 30

The world's longest trial begins in Hong Kong, where 14 South Vietnamese are accused of murdering 24 North Vietnamese. The trial would end on November 29, 1994.

DECEMBER 1

"Long Island Lolita" Amy Fisher is sentenced to 5 to 15 years for shooting Mary Jo Buttafuoco, her lover's wife.

DECEMBER 2

Human rights activist Elie Wiesel visits Bosnia and talks to Serbian leader Slobodan Milosevic about the violence in Yugoslavia.

DECEMBER 3

The UN Security Council passes a resolution to send a coalition of peacekeepers to Somalia to distribute humanitarian aid.

DECEMBER 4

President Bush dispatches 28,000 U.S. troops to Somalia to intervene in the Somali civil war.

DECEMBER 5

In the SEC Championship game, held at Legion Field in Birmingham, Alabama, the Alabama Crimson Tide defeats the Florida Gators 28–21.

DECEMBER 6

Extremist Hindu activists destroy the Babri Masjid mosque in Ayodhya, India, leading to widespread communal violence.

DECEMBER 7

The *Galileo* spacecraft passes the moon's North Pole.

DECEMBER 8

NBC announces the final season of *Cheers.*

DECEMBER 9

Prince Charles and Princess Diana
publicly announce their separation.

With the release of its 180 line of Macintosh PowerBooks in October of 1992, Apple
introduces a portable computer with all the power and capabilities of a desktop model.
(The PowerBook 180c, released in 1993, is shown here.)

DECEMBER 10

The *Chicago Tribune* reports that the purple dinosaur named Barney is becoming a craze among kids, with stores already selling out of Barney toys.

DECEMBER 11

Making the news in *Entertainment Weekly* are John Candy, Dr. Dre, George Michael, and Debbie Gibson.

DECEMBER 12

Julia Kurotchkina of Russia is crowned the 42nd Miss World.

DECEMBER 13

The FCC fines Infinity Broadcasting $600,000 over the *Howard Stern Show*.

DECEMBER 14

Time magazine's cover story looks at the strife in Somalia.

DECEMBER 15

Pioneering black tennis player Arthur Ashe is named
Sports Illustrated's Sportsman of the Year.

DECEMBER 16

In Los Angeles, California, singer
Rick James ("Super Freak") and his
girlfriend remain in custody on
assault charges. James was out on
bail from a separate assault charge.

DECEMBER 17

The *Los Angeles Times* reports that ABC will
change its Thursday-night lineup,
dropping Delta Burke's show *Delta* and
bringing back Andy Griffith's *Matlock*.

DECEMBER 18

Celebrities making the news in *Entertainment
Weekly* include Shannen Doherty,
Arnold Schwarzenegger, and
40-year-old animated character Gumby.

DECEMBER 19

English music group Duran Duran, a sensation in the 1980s, releases its single "Ordinary World," which would revive the band's popularity and go on to win the Ivor Novello Award.

DECEMBER 20

Slobodan Milosevic is reelected president of Serbia.

DECEMBER 21

Time magazine's cover story looks at Operation Restore Hope, the U.S. effort to aid Somalia.

DECEMBER 22

Popular movies for the week include *A Few Good Men,* Disney's *Aladdin, The Bodyguard,* and *Home Alone 2: Lost in New York.*

DECEMBER 23

The *New York Times* reports on the conflict brewing at NBC over the *Tonight Show,* as Jay Leno is threatened with being replaced by David Letterman.

DECEMBER 24

President Bush pardons Caspar Weinberger
of his involvement in the Iran-Contra affair.

Astronomer Galileo Galilei (1564–1642) receives an apology from Pope John Paul II and the Vatican on October 31 for his trial during the Inquisition.

DECEMBER 25

Entertainment Weekly lists the year's best books, which include
All the Pretty Horses (Cormac McCarthy), *Jazz* (Toni Morrison),
and *The Secret History* (Donna Tartt). Among the books it
deems the worst of the year is Ivana Trump's *For Love Alone*.

DECEMBER 26

New York Jets announcer Marty Glickman retires.

DECEMBER 27

Grammy Award–winning singer, actor, and musician Harry Connick Jr.
is arrested in New York at JFK airport after reporting that his luggage
contains an unloaded 9 mm pistol, a Christmas gift. In lieu of serving
time, he agrees to make a public service announcement about gun safety.

DECEMBER 28

Time magazine's cover story poses the question:
"What Does Science Tell Us About God?"

DECEMBER 29

New York governor Mario Cuomo grants clemency to Jean Harris, who had been
convicted of killing her lover, Dr. Herman Tarnower, creator of the Scarsdale Diet.

DECEMBER 30

In the Holiday Bowl, the Hawaii Rainbow Warriors face off with the Illinois Fighting Illini in San Diego, California. Hawaii wins, 27–17.

DECEMBER 31

The *Washington Post* reports the death of Ling-Ling, the female member of the pair of giant pandas in the National Zoo in Washington, D.C. Along with her mate Hsing-Hsing, the panda had been a gift from the government of China following President Nixon's landmark visit to that country.

Under a United Nations mandate, the United States–led Unified Task Force lands in Somalia on December 4, hoping to quell chaos long enough to bring humanitarian aid to the area.

Paul Simon (shown here in a photo from 2011) plays the first concert in South Africa by a Western artist following the lifting of the United Nations cultural boycott in place since the 1960s.

Pop Culture in 1992

Popular culture in 1992 was particularly rich. We had the Olympic Games and talk-show wars. We had clever, timely scripted television like *Mad About You* and *Murphy Brown*, but also the first of what would become a dominant television revolution, reality TV. Music-video network MTV introduced the groundbreaking series *The Real World*, which threw photogenic, volatile young adults into a communal living situation and filmed the resulting pyrotechnics. It was instantly addictive, and paved the way for such reality TV phenoms as *Survivor*, *Big Brother*, and *Fear Factor*.

On the big screen, Disney's *Aladdin* transported us to "A Whole New World," but for many audience members it was Robin Williams's chameleonic, pop-culture-savvy Genie that made the story come alive. At the Academy Awards, the big winner was the film adaptation of Thomas Harris's thriller *The Silence of the Lambs*, which had made us cheer perversely for a serial killer, played unforgettably by Oscar winner Anthony Hopkins. The Academy Awards were also notable for containing the first animated nominee for Best Picture, Disney's instant classic *Beauty and the Beast*. (The Oscar telecast included animated guest appearances by the two leads.)

Works of fiction we were reading in 1992 ranged from the lyrical romance of *The Bridges of Madison County* to the Pulitzer Prize–winning graphic novel about a Holocaust survivor, *Maus: A Survivor's Tale*. Above all, 1992 was a year marked by variety of choice—a year like none other.

Garth Brooks (shown here in 2010) leads a global country music explosion and wins the Country Music Association's Entertainer of the Year award.

Top five male baby names:
1. Michael
2. Christopher
3. Matthew
4. Joshua
5. Andrew

Top five female baby names:
1. Ashley
2. Jessica
3. Amanda
4. Brittany
5. Sarah

Five television shows that began in 1992:

Mad About You, NBC

Melrose Place, Fox

Highlander: The Series, CBS

The Real World, MTV

X-Men, Fox

Five television shows that ended in 1992:

The Cosby Show

The Golden Girls

Growing Pains

Who's the Boss

Night Court

Popular books:

She's Come Undone, by Wally Lamb

The Pelican Brief, by John Grisham

Sex, by Madonna

All the Pretty Horses, by Cormac McCarthy

The Bridges of Madison County, by Robert James Waller

Top five highest-grossing movies:
1. *Aladdin* ($504,050,291)
2. *The Bodyguard* ($420,945,720)
3. *Home Alone 2: Lost in New York* ($358,994,850)
4. *Basic Instinct* ($352,927,224)
5. *Lethal Weapon 3* ($321,731,527)

The Freddie Mercury Tribute Concert for AIDS Awareness held on April 20 honors the memory of the frontman of Queen (shown in 1978), raises funds, and brings worldwide attention to the AIDS epidemic.

Sports champions:

Major League Baseball: Toronto Blue Jays

National Football League: Washington Redskins

National Basketball Association: Chicago Bulls

National Hockey League: Pittsburgh Penguins

Indianapolis 500 Champion: Al Unser Jr.

Horse racing champions:

Kentucky Derby: Lil E. Tee

Preakness Stakes: Pine Bluff

Belmont Stakes: A.P. Indy

Medal count for the Summer Olympic Games (Barcelona, Spain):

1. Unified Team (former Soviet Union): 45 Gold, 38 Silver, 29 Bronze

2. United States: 37 Gold, 34 Silver, 37 Bronze

3. Germany: 33 Gold, 21 Silver, 28 Bronze

4. China: 16 Gold, 22 Silver, 16 Bronze

5. Cuba: 14 Gold, 6 Silver, 11 Bronze

Medal Count for the Winter Olympic Games (Albertville, France):

1. Germany: 10 Gold, 10 Silver 6 Bronze

2. Unified Team (former Soviet Union): 9 Gold, 6 Silver, 8 Bronze

3. Norway: 9 Gold, 6 Silver 5 Bronze

4. Austria: 6 Gold, 7 Silver, 8 Bronze

5. United States: 5 Gold, 4 Silver, 2 Bronze

New products:

Windows 3.1 (Microsoft)

Microsoft Works (Microsoft)

Video Phone (AT&T)

Nicotine patch

Academy Awards:

Best Picture: *The Silence of the Lambs*

Best Director: Jonathan Demme, *The Silence of the Lambs*

Best Actor: Anthony Hopkins, *The Silence of the Lambs*

Best Actress: Jodie Foster, *The Silence of the Lambs*

Best Supporting Actor: Jack Palance, *City Slickers*

Best Supporting Actress: Mercedes Ruehl, *The Fisher King*

Best Original Screenplay: *Thelma & Louise,* Callie Khouri

Best Adapted Screenplay: *The Silence of the Lambs,* Ted Tally

Diva Whitney Houston is everywhere in 1992, as she stars in the hit film *The Bodyguard*, has an international blockbuster singing "I Will Always Love You" for its soundtrack, and, on July 18, marries R&B star Bobby Brown.

Best Original Song: "Beauty and the Beast" from *Beauty and the Beast*
    (music by Alan Menken, lyrics by Howard Ashman)
Irving G. Thalberg Memorial Award: George Lucas

Golden Globe Awards:
Best Picture, Drama: *Bugsy*
Best Picture, Musical or Comedy: *Beauty and the Beast*
Best Director: Oliver Stone, *JFK*
Best Actor, Drama: Nick Nolte, *The Prince of Tides*
Best Actor, Musical or Comedy: Robin Williams, *The Fisher King*
Best Actress, Drama: Jodie Foster, *The Silence of the Lambs*
Best Actress, Musical or Comedy: Bette Midler, *For the Boys*
Best Supporting Actor: Jack Palance, *City Slickers*
Best Supporting Actress: Mercedes Ruehl, *The Fisher King*
Best Actor, Drama Series: Scott Bakula, *Quantum Leap*
Best Actor, Musical or Comedy Series: Burt Reynolds, *Evening Shade*
Best Actress, Drama Series: Angela Lansbury, *Murder, She Wrote*
Best Actress, Musical or Comedy Series: Candice Bergen, *Murphy Brown*
Best Series, Drama: *Northern Exposure*
Best Series, Musical or Comedy: *Brooklyn Bridge*
Best Supporting Actor, Series, Miniseries, or TV Film: Louis Gossett Jr., *The Josephine Baker Story*
Best Supporting Actress, Series, Miniseries, or TV Film: Amanda Donohoe, *L.A. Law*

Pulitzer Prizes:
Fiction: *A Thousand Acres* by Jane Smiley
Drama: *The Kentucky Cycle* by Robert Schenkkan
History: *The Fate of Liberty: Abraham Lincoln and Civil Liberties* by Mark E. Neely
Biography or Autobiography: *Fortunate Son: The Healing of a Vietnam Vet* by Lewis B. Puller
Poetry: *Selected Poems* by James Tate
General Nonfiction: *The Prize: The Epic Quest For Oil, Money & Power* by Daniel Yergin
Music: *The Face of the Night, The Heart of the Dark* by Wayne Peterson
Special Citations—Letters: Art Spiegelman for *Maus: A Survivor's Tale.*

Credits and Acknowledgments

Peyton Smith-Hopman wrote text; Holly Musgrove selected images. Individual image credits are as follows.

Chapter 1. Selena Gomez—Glenn Francis, www.PacificProDigital.com. Demi Lovato—Angela George. Nick Jonas—AlBBie905. Miley Cyrus—Sgt. Michael Connors.

Chapter 2. Chrysler—Print Advertisement/Alden Jewell. Gas station—U.S. Navy Photo by Photographer's Mate 2nd Class Susan Cornell. Barry Bonds—Jim Accordino.

Chapter 3. Bill Clinton—Bob McNeely, the White House. Ford truck ad—Print Advertisement/Alden Jewell. Candice Bergen and Joe Regalbuto—Alan Light. Nirvana–Feral78; http://www.flickr.com/photos/emmettgrrrl/6213509717/in/photostream. The Bushes and Yeltsin—David Valdez, NARA. Haley Heritage Square—Joelk75. Kristi Yamaguchi—the White House. Milli Vanilli—Alan Light. Samuel Reshevsky—Kadel & Herbert. Wal-Mart—strangelv. *Isaac Asimov Science Fiction Magazine*—Chris Drumm. L.A. riots—Ripper777. *Endeavour* maiden voyage—NASA. Lawrence Welk—Wikimedia Commons. *Glacier Girl*—U.S. Air Force photo by Tech. Sgt. Ben Bloker. Johnny Carson—Alan Light. Jay Leno and Barack Obama—White House (Pete Souza). Oscar De La Hoya—Jane Davees. Hurricane Andrew aftermath—NOAA. Anthony Perkins and Charmian Carr—Wikimedia Commons. Mae Jemison—NASA. Apple Powerbook 180—ABerham Nuñez. Galileo Galilei—painting by Justus Sustermans, 1636. U.S. military in Somalia—John Martinez Pavliga.

Chapter 4. Paul Simon—Matthew Straubmuller. Garth Brooks—the White House. Freddie Mercury—Carl Lender. Whitney Houston—PH2 Mark Kettenhofen.